WORLD TALES

The extraordinary coincidence of stories told in all times, in all places

ISBN 978-1-78479-232-9

First published 1979
Published in this edition 2015

In association with The Idries Shah Foundation

The ISF Collectors' Library

Tales of A Parrot and Other Stories

The Happiest Man in The World
and Other Stories

The Food of Paradise
and Other Stories

The Water of Life and Other Stories

The Land Where Time Stood Still
and Other Stories

This special edition of *World Tales*
is limited to five hundred copies.

Of which this is number 196.

The Land Where Time Stood Still and Other Stories

VOLUME V

Collected by
IDRIES SHAH

The ISF Collectors' Library

'That lurking air of hidden meanings and immemorial mythical signs which we find in some fables, recalling a people, wise and childish at once, who had built up a theory of the world ages before Aesop was born.'
— Ernest Rhys, 1925

'The content of folklore is metaphysics. Our inability to see this is due primarily to our abysmal ignorance of metaphysics and its technical terms.'
— A. K. Coomaraswamy

'The folktale is the primer of the picture-language of the soul.'
—Joseph Campbell

'They (tales) appeal to our rational and irrational instincts, to our visions and dreams… The race is richer in human and cultural values for its splendid heritage of old magic tales.'
— Dr Leonard W. Roberts

Introduction

It is quite usual to find collections of tales arranged according to language or country: *Tales of Belgium*, *Stories from the German*, or *Legends from the Indian Peoples*; some such titles must have met your eye at one time or another. It all looks very tidy, scientific even; and the study of stories is indeed a part of scholarly research.

But the deeper you go into things, the more mysterious, exciting, baffling they become. How can it be that the same story is found in Scotland and also in pre-Columbian America? Was the story of Aladdin and his Wonderful Lamp really taken from Wales (where it has been found) to the ancient East; and, if so, by whom and when? A classical Japanese narrative is part of the gypsy repertoire in Europe; where shall we pigeonhole it in national terms?

I have selected and place before you a collection of tales of which one at least goes back to the ancient Egyptian of several thousand years ago. It is presented here not to impress the reader with its age, but because it is entertaining, and also because, although the Pharaohs died out many centuries ago, this tale is recited by people all over the world who know nothing of its origins. This form of culture remains when nations, languages and faiths have long since died.

There is an almost uncanny persistence and

durability in the tale which cannot be accounted for in the present state of knowledge. Not only does it constantly appear in different incarnations which can be mapped – as the Tar-Baby story carried from Africa to America, and medieval Arabian stories from the Saracens in Sicily to the Italy of today – but from time to time remarkable collections are assembled and enjoy a phenomenal vogue: after which they lapse and are reborn, perhaps in another culture, perhaps centuries later: to delight, attract, thrill, captivate yet another audience.

Such was the great *Panchatantra*, the Far Eastern collection of tales for the education of Indian princes; the Jataka Buddhist birth-stories believed to date back two and a half thousand years; the *Thousand and One Nights*, known as 'The Mother of Tales'. Later came the collections of Straparola, Boccaccio, Chaucer and Shakespeare, and a dozen others which now form the very basis of the classical literature of Europe and Asia.

This book contains stories from all of these collections, and many more: because there is a certain basic fund of human fictions which recur, again and again, and never seem to lose their compelling attraction. Many traditional tales have a surface meaning (perhaps just a socially uplifting one) and a secondary, inner significance, which is rarely glimpsed consciously, but which nevertheless acts powerfully upon our minds. Tales have always been used, so far as we can judge, for spiritual as well as social purposes: and as parables with more or less obvious meanings this use is familiar to most people today. But, as Professor Geoffrey Parrinder says of the myth, 'its inner truth was realised when the participant was transported into the realm of the sacred and eternal.'*

Perhaps above all the tale fulfils the function not of escape but of hope. The suspending of ordinary constraints helps people to reclaim optimism and to fuel the imagination with energy for the attainment of goals: whether moral or material. Maxim Gorky realised this when he wrote: 'In tales people fly through the air on a magic carpet, walk in seven-league boots, build castles overnight; the tales opened up for me a new world where some free and all-fearless power reigned and inspired in me a dream of a better life.'

When relatively recent collectors of tales, such as Hans Christian Andersen, the Brothers Grimm, Perrault and others made their selections, they both re-established certain powerful tales in our cultures and left out others from the very vast riches of the world reservoir of stories. Paradoxically, by their very success in imprinting Cinderella, Puss-in-Boots and Beauty and the Beast anew for the modern reader (they are all very ancient tales, widely dispersed) they directed attention away from some of the most wonderful and arresting stories which did not feature

* G. Parrinder, Foreword to *Pears Encyclopaedia of Myths and Legends*, London 1976, p.10.

in their collections. Many of these stories are re-presented here.

Working for thirty-five years among the written and oral sources of our world heritage in tales, one feels a truly living element in them which is startlingly evident when one isolates the 'basic' stories: the ones which tend to have travelled farthest, to have featured in the largest number of classical collections, to have inspired great writers of the past and present.

One becomes aware, by this contact with the fund of tradition which constantly cries out to be projected anew, that the story in some elusive way is the basic form and inspiration. Thought or style, characterisation and belief, didactic and nationality, all recede to give place to the tale which feels almost as if it is demanding to be reborn through one's efforts. And yet those efforts themselves, in some strange way, are experienced as no more than the relatively poor expertise of the humblest midwife. It is the tale itself, when it emerges, which is king.

Erskine Caldwell, no less, has felt a similar power in the story, and is well aware of its primacy over mere thought of philosophy: 'A writer,' he says (*Atlantic Monthly*, July 1958) 'is not a great mind, he's not a great thinker, he's not a great philosopher, he's a story-teller.'

Idries Shah

Note: This is the full introduction as it appeared in the original version of *World Tales*

Contents

The Lost Camel

There is an ancient Islamic saying, 'Faith is the lost camel of the Believer', and it has been said that this is an allusion to this very tale. In such a sense, of course, the lost camel symbolises faith, and its traces are held to be visible to certain specially endowed individuals and not to others.

The version given here, however, is on the political level: where the King realises that people who can observe signs which others cannot would be useful at Court, and he employs them accordingly.

The story is also used in some Eastern circles, in a more abbreviated form, to test the reactions of the audience, much as a modern psychologist would, to discover what the mentality of the hearer is through what interpretation he puts on the story. There are many tales-within-a-tale extant which record how various potential disciples have reacted to the story. Some have said that it constitutes a sort of early detective story; others that it underlines the existence of specially endowed individuals who roam this earth performing perceptive functions about which most people are unaware; in some stories the plot forms the basis of an unjust accusation of theft – the travellers know too much about the camel not to be thought its thieves. One telling ends with the interpretation that 'things are not what they seem'; and another is used to encourage children to develop their powers of observation for personal advantage later in life.

Most of the instrumental and interpretative functions of the folktale have tended to be overlooked in the literature, which still usually concentrates upon origins, upon fragmentary beliefs enshrined in the tales, and upon the light which is cast by plots and treatments on the attitudes of the peoples among whom the story is told.

In India at the time of Alakapuri's greatest power, there dwelt in it a great king whose name was Alakesa, and he was famous for all the riches which land and sea can yield.

During his reign the cow and the tiger drank side by side from the same pool, and the parrot and the kite, the Indian scavenger bird, laid their eggs in the same nest. Rain refreshed the soil when it was needed, and all King Alakesa's subjects lived like brothers in peace, plenty and happiness.

Now, there was in Alakapuri a rich merchant who lost his camel one day. He searched for it for a long time without success, until he reached another city, called Mathurapuri, the king of which was named Mathuresa. There were four ministers of that country, called Bodhadita, Bodhachandra, Bodhavyapka, and Bodhavibishana.

For some reason, they had become dissatisfied with their positions at court, and decided to quit the city.

As they journeyed along, they observed the tracks of a camel, and each made some remark about the animal, judging by its footsteps and other indications on the road.

Presently they met the merchant who was searching for his camel.

'Masters,' said he, 'have you met a camel anywhere in the direction from which you have come?'

One wise man asked, 'Was it lame in one of its legs?'

'Yes, indeed,' said he.

'And was it not blind in one eye?' asked the second wise man. 'The right eye?'

'Yes, it was,' said he.

'Was its tail unusually short?' asked the third.

'Yes, yes, then you have seen it?' exclaimed the merchant.

'Was it not suffering from colic, too?' interposed the fourth wise man.

'Yes, yes, it was! But, where is it now?' asked the merchant, in some distress.

'We have not seen it,' the first courtier said, 'but we have observed its progress along the road.'

'Observed it? But please explain,' cried the merchant.

'We cannot possibly tell you where it is, we are all now on our way to the court of King Alakesa,' replied the traveller. 'But if you will come with us we will give you the explanation of our findings.'

So, the merchant had no choice but to go with them to the King, Alakesa, and complain that the four men had stolen his beast and hidden it somewhere.

The King was sure that the men must know something about the whereabouts of the camel, since they had given a complete description of it.

'You are all threatened with my displeasure,' said

he, 'if you do not tell me the whole truth. According to what you shall now say, I will make judgment.'

The first traveller said, 'I noticed, when first seeing the footprints of the camel on the side of the road, that one of the footmarks was deficient, therefore I concluded that the animal was lame.'

'Good,' said the King. 'And you, Bodhachandra, what have you to say?'

'I noticed that the leaves on the left side of the road had been snapped or torn off,' said the second courtier, 'therefore it was obvious that the camel was blind of his right eye.'

The third said, 'I saw drops of blood on the road which I conjectured had fallen from the bites of gnats or flies, therefore I thought the camel's tail was shorter than usual, as it could not brush the pests away.'

The fourth said, 'I observed that whilst the forefeet of the animal were planted firmly on the ground the hind ones seemed scarcely to have touched it, whence I guessed that they were contracted by pain in the body of the camel.'

When the King heard these explanations he was struck by the wisdom of the four men, and the logic of their replies.

'Well spoken,' said he, 'and I will compensate you, Merchant, for the loss of your camel, as it obviously will not be found easily.

'You four young men from Mathurapuri I beg to

remain here and become my counsellors, for I have great need of your intelligence.'

And so they came to the court of the great King, becoming ministers of great importance.

The Beggar and the Gazelle

One of the best-known stories in the English-speaking world is 'Puss in Boots', which came to Britain through the translations of Perrault's 'Le Chat Botté', of 1697. Perrault, writing as he did for the French court, prettified this story; and the current story-book form is much distorted. The story is an Eastern one, and appeared in Italy as early as the 16th century. It was known in a French literary translation from Straparola a century before Perrault took it over. The tale has annoyed many people in the West, because they have disliked (as did Madame de Maintenon) its supposed lack of a moral. On the surface, of course, it looks as if a beggar (or a young miller without a penny, as in the 'Puss in Boots' version) has no right to advantages obtained for him by a cat, through trickery. But in the Eastern telling it is easier to see that the animal stands for the fate which constantly gives humanity (in spite of its unworthiness) great opportunities. The ingratitude of the main figure is thus characteristic of man's forgetfulness of a debt. The defection of the Princess symbolises the withdrawal of

the advantages which subsist, according to this idea, only when appreciated by a worthwhile person.

The story is well known in the Middle East, where the man is known as Hamadani, and the variant given here is current in substantially similar form in Zanzibar and East Africa, as well as in the Near East.

ONCE UPON A time there was a poor beggar who slept upon the outside oven of a rich man's kitchen. One morning he was awakened by the cries of a vendor who was calling, 'Gazelles! Gazelles! Buy my fine miniature gazelles!'

The beggar said, 'There is no one awake at this hour in the rich man's house. Cease from your noise until a more civilised hour, brother.'

The gazelle-seller, who had several of the poor creatures in a cage on top of a donkey cart, replied, 'Would you like to buy one of these fine gazelles?'

'I have only a handful of coppers,' said the beggar. 'What would I do with a gazelle, anyway?' And he climbed down off the oven to talk to the gazelle-seller.

At that moment one of the small animals poked its head out of the cage and said in a low voice to the beggar, whose name was Mustapha, 'Buy me, and you will not be sorry.'

Mustapha was so astonished that he said to the gazelle-seller, 'Here is all I have in the world – three copper coins. Can I buy this gazelle with its head out of the cage for that?'

'Take it and be blessed!' cried the man, and released the gazelle. 'As I shall otherwise only have to feed the thing I shall let it go for whatever you can give me.' Then he closed the cage again, took three coppers from Mustapha, and went on his way to the nearest coffee-house.

'Well,' said Mustapha to the gazelle, 'what about it? I have bought you, and now I have nothing left in the world, until I can get something more sitting on the steps of the mosque at the time of the midday prayer.'

'You will not regret buying me,' said the gazelle, 'for I shall make your fortune.'

'How is that?' cried Mustapha, 'and what shall I do next?'

'Do nothing, simply stay here until I return,' said the gazelle, and it trotted away.

The tattered beggar scratched his head. He would probably never see the wretched animal again, he thought. How did he allow himself to be so deluded as to give his three copper coins for a talking gazelle? Probably the creature was bewitched, and might bring him bad luck. So ruminating, he sat down again on the oven to wait until the rich man's servants woke, hoping that then perhaps they would throw out some food that he could eat.

Meanwhile, the gazelle ran on until it reached the tent of a noble sheikh. It bowed to him and said, 'O Sheikh of a Thousand Tents, I am the slave of a great and noble merchant, whose caravan has just been attacked and plundered by thieves. Could you please send some clothes for him to put on, so that he may not have to appear before you completely naked when he comes to pay you a visit?'

‘Certainly, good gazelle,’ said the Sheikh. ‘My servant shall give you a white linen shirt and a robe of the finest camel-hair to take to your master. And when he has recovered from his shock, let him come here to my encampment, so that I may cause a sheep to be roasted in his honour.’

So the gazelle thanked the Sheikh and said, ‘I was to bring you this emerald in payment of any clothes which you might send, as my master does not wish to accept your kindness for nothing.’ Thereupon the gazelle placed an emerald without flaw at the feet of the Sheikh, and bounded away with the clothes upon its back.

The Sheikh was delighted at the value of the gift, and resolved that if the man did appear he would offer him the hand of his daughter, for he was apparently a person of great substance.

The gazelle went back to Mustapha and said, ‘Look, I have brought you clothes from a rich sheikh. Cast off your rags, bathe in the river, and put on these magnificent garments.’

The beggar was amazed, and said, ‘How in the world did you manage to do this? Never in my life have I seen such beautiful clothes.’

‘Do as I tell you,’ said the gazelle, ‘and I shall get you a rich wife as well. Did you not give me back my liberty by buying me from the man who had put me in a cage?’

The long and the short of it was that the clothes transformed the beggar into a man who could sit in a royal court without shame.

'Now, follow me,' said the gazelle, and trotted off into a ruined building. 'Look under the third brick on the left and you will see a treasure.'

Sure enough, as Mustapha lifted the brick he saw the gleam of gold and precious stones in a cavity below. He filled his pockets and his money-belt, until he had as much as he could carry.

'What a piece of luck!' cried the beggar. 'I shall never have to go without anything for the rest of my days.'

'Not if you marry into the family of the Sheikh of a Thousand Tents,' said the gazelle. 'Buy yourself a horse, and boots, and we shall set out for the noble Sheikh's oasis at once.'

An hour later Mustapha, mounted on a beautiful white horse, followed the gazelle as it sped along like the wind before him. Soon they reached a dip in the sand, and in the distance, beside some tall palm trees, were some black tents.

'Wait here,' said the gazelle, 'until I come for you; and remember that you are now the Sheikh Abu Zakat, a rich merchant whose caravan has been set upon by thieves and plundered.'

'I understand,' said Mustapha. 'I shall stay here until you return.'

The gazelle then descended into the valley of the oasis and, presenting himself to the Sheikh of a Thousand Tents, let fall a priceless ruby without flaw at his feet, saying, 'My master, the noble Sheikh Abu Zakat, sends you blessings and peace, and requests that he may call upon you at once, to thank you for the clothes you sent him after his recent misfortune. In the meantime, here is a small token of his regard which he wishes to give to your daughter as a mark of his respect.'

'Excellent gazelle!' cried the Sheikh. 'Let your master hasten here as fast as he can, for I am eager to meet him, and he should start thinking of himself as my son-in-law from this moment.'

The gazelle returned to the Sheikh Abu Zakat and acquainted him of what the Sheikh of a Thousand Tents had said, and soon the one-time beggar and the rich and venerable Sheikh were sitting together drinking coffee like old friends. By nightfall, when the sheep had been roasted and eaten, the Sheikh of a Thousand Tents came to the delicate subject of his daughter. 'My son,' said he, placing his hand on Sheikh Abu Zakat's arm, 'I am glad that I have kept my daughter unmarried until you came along; for I can think of no more suitable match for her. I shall arrange for the marriage rites to be solemnised tomorrow, and she shall come to you with her servants and her finery all complete.'

At this news the Sheikh Abu Zakat was delighted and thanked his lucky stars for bringing him such fortune.

Next day, at the wedding, he was congratulated by every member of the tribe, who each piled gifts before the happy pair. The bridal feast went on for twelve hours, and at last they were led to a black tent hung with rare carpets and decorated with lamps of burnished brass set with coral. While they slept the gazelle lay across the threshold, keeping watch.

The months passed, and the tribe moved to another oasis, so the Sheikh of a Thousand Tents gave his daughter and new son-in-law his palace in the desert to live in until his return. There were tinkling fountains in blue-tiled courtyards, carved wooden balconies, vast rooms with painted pillars. The Sheikh Abu Zakat became more and more conceited, and forgot completely what he owed to the gazelle. He spent all day playing knucklebones with his friends.

One day the gazelle went to its mistress and said, 'Lady, ask my master if he will give me a bowl of dates and honey, prepared with his own hands, for I am feeling ill, and fear that I may die.'

So the girl went to her husband and said, 'Peace be upon you, Husband. Please give the gazelle a bowl of dates and honey prepared with your own hands as it is ill and fears that it may die.'

And the man answered, 'Foolish one, do not worry about the animal. Did I not buy it for only a few pence? Take no notice, and leave me to my game of knucklebones.'

Then the girl went back to the gazelle, which was lying on the ground looking very weak and thin, and said, 'I cannot get your master to come. Shall I prepare you the mixture myself so that you will get better?'

The gazelle said, 'No, mistress, thank you, I would rather that my master did it. Please go back to him and beg him for my sake to do as I ask, or I shall die.'

So she ran back to Sheikh Abu Zakat and said, 'Come quickly: the gazelle begs you to do as it asks, or indeed it will die, for it is now so weak and thin, lying on the ground.'

But again her husband would not do anything, and told her to go to the gazelle and give it a bowl of milk herself.

When the girl got back to where the gazelle was lying she saw its eyes were very dull, and when she had told it the Sheikh was not coming, it dropped its head and died.

That night, lying in his luxurious palace, the man who had been a beggar said to his wife, 'What happened to the gazelle? You did not come back to tell me.'

And she answered sadly, 'It died, and I am so

grieved at the way you disregarded the poor creature's pleas that I have decided when my father comes back I shall return to his tents, for I no longer love you.'

'Foolish woman!' cried the Sheikh. 'Go to sleep, and in the morning you will have forgotten all about this matter.' Within a few moments he was snoring.

In the middle of the night he had a dream. He thought he saw the gazelle again, and its eyes were very sad. 'Why did you not bring me a bowl of dates and honey when I begged you to do so? Had you forgotten that you owed all your good fortune to me? I was grateful because you bought my liberty back for me, why could you not show me one act of kindness when I was in need?'

'I asked my wife to take you a bowl of milk!' cried the Sheikh Abu Zakat, feeling suddenly very ashamed of himself.

'It was not the same thing,' said the gazelle, faintly, and it disappeared.

In a great fright the Sheikh Abu Zakat sat up, and found himself Mustapha the beggar again, dressed in tatters, sitting against the outdoor oven of a rich man's house in the moonlight.

The Apple on the Boy's Head

William Tell is said, in 1296, to have shot an apple from the head of his son when an enraged Governor challenged him to do so for refusing to salute his hat, symbol of alien authority. The story, however, is not related of Tell until 1499 AD, two centuries after the incident. But it does appear in the Old Norse Vilkina Saga and, three hundred years before William Tell, in the Saga of Saint Olof. A hundred years ago the Swiss themselves decided that the story was legendary, though a man named Freudenberger had been burned alive by the Canton of Uri in the early eighteenth century for claiming the legend to be of Danish origin. Tradition indeed ascribes the arrow incident to Palnatoki, bodyguard of Harold Bluetooth, in 950 AD. Some discomfort has been occasioned by the statement (in the Icelandic Saga) that the original apple-target idea was suggested by a Christian saint who wished to convert the heathen hero Eindridi.

Apart from these considerations, the tale itself might well be seen to highlight the problems of category definitions in the field of tales. Is it, for instance, a myth, relating to the Nordic gods, said to be of Hodr in the Edda? Is it a legend, of William of Cloudisley of Britain, as it appears in the 'Ballad of Adam Bell'? As a 'fairy tale', it belongs among the Märchen, to amuse; but as a didactic fable, it would inculcate principles. Some, on the other hand, see it as an allegory, that is 'fabulous, but indicating some history'.

It does not help matters that this fascinating idea is very common to others than (as Sir George Dasent has claimed) 'the whole Aryan race'. The Turks, Mongols and Samoyeds all attribute it to their own heroes. I was last told it as a true local story by a Cypriot taxi-driver in Paphos, the legendary birthplace of Venus. As the Swiss William Tell variety is easily found and known to many people, here for comparison is the version from the Vilkina Saga, *three centuries before Tell's time.*

A CERTAIN PALNATOKI, for some time among King Harold's bodyguard, had made his bravery odious to very many of his fellow-soldiers by the zeal with which he surpassed them in the discharge of his duty.

This man once, when talking tipsily over his cups, had boasted that he was so skilled an archer that he could hit the smallest apple placed a long way off on a stick, at the first shot; which talk, caught up at first by the ears of backbiters, soon came to the hearing of the King.

Now mark how the wickedness of the King turned the confidence of the father to the peril of the son, by commanding that this dearest pledge of his life should be placed, instead of the stick; with a threat that, unless the author of this promise could strike off the apple at the first flight of the arrow, he should pay the penalty of his empty boasting by the loss of his head.

The King's command forced the soldier to perform more than he had promised, and what he had said, reported by the tongue of slanderers, bound him to accomplish what he had not said.

Nor did his sterling courage, though caught in the snare of slander, suffer him to lay aside his firmness of heart; nay, he accepted the trial the more readily because it was hard. So Palnatoki warned the boy urgently, when he took his stand, to await the coming of the hurtling arrow with calm ears and unbent head; lest by a slight turn of his body he should defeat the practised skill of the bowman. And, taking further counsel to prevent his fear, he turned away his face, lest he should be scared at the sight of the weapon. Then, taking three arrows from the quiver, he struck the mark given him with the first he fitted to the string. But, if chance had brought the head of the boy before the shaft, no doubt the penalty of the son would have recoiled to the peril of the father, and the swerving of the shaft that struck the boy would have linked them both in common ruin.

I am in doubt, then, whether to admire more the courage of the father or the temper of the son, of whom the one by skill in his art avoided being the slayer of his child, while the other by patience of mind and quietness of body saved himself alive, and spared the natural affection of his father. Nay, the youthful frame strengthened the aged heart, and showed as much courage in awaiting the arrow as the father skill in launching it.

But Palnatoki, when asked by the King why he had taken more arrows from the quiver, when it had been settled that he should only try the fortune of the bow *once*, made answer:

'That I might avenge on thee the swerving of the first by the points of the rest, lest perchance my innocence might have been punished, while your violence escaped scot-free.'

The Boots of Hunain

There is a Middle Eastern proverb, 'The boots of Hunain', referring to something which is not such a bargain as it seems to be. This story, in its essentials and with remarkable fidelity of incident, is found all over the world. There is a Hebrew version, in which a Jewish cobbler outsmarts a desert Arab who has been rude to him; a Gaelic one from the Highlands of Scotland, and a Norwegian tale featuring a master-thief. The modern Greek and German tales with this plot closely resemble the one from Bangladesh, while in England the tale is positively stated to have happened to 'A butcher in Lewes, Essex' (though Lewes is in the county of Sussex). The following is the presentation found in Ibn Khallikan's monumental Wafayat, *written in the thirteenth century, the first Arabian dictionary of biography. Its author himself came from a Central Asian family, where the story may have been current.*

THERE WAS ONCE a desert Arab who rode into town and saw a pair of boots offered for sale in the market. He went into the shop and made an offer for them, but Hunain the shoemaker stuck to his price, and in the end the infuriated bedouin stamped out of the shop. 'The price you ask is equal to the value of my camel,' he snorted.

Now the shoemaker was deeply affronted by the behaviour and language of this Arab, and decided that he would not let him get away with such insults. The Arab had mounted his camel and started along the trail towards the tents of his tribe. The shoemaker, knowing from where his would-be customer had come, picked up the boots and went by short-cuts to a point which the Arab would have to pass eventually. There he placed one boot on the sand.

Then the shoemaker went a mile or more further along the road and dropped the other boot, hiding himself to watch what happened, for he had a plan.

Presently the Arab came along, and saw the first boot lying on the ground. He said to himself, 'That is one of the boots of Hunain, the cobbler; if only it was a pair, I would be able to get down and take them away for nothing.' And he went on his way. After all, what was the use of one boot?

Soon afterwards, of course, the Arab came upon the second boot. He thought, 'What a pity I did not take up the first one – then I would have had a pair.'

Then it occurred to him that he might go back for the first boot, then he would have them both.

The bedouin was some way from his own tents, and did not want to tire his camel, so he hobbled it and ran back to the place where he had seen the first boot.

The shoemaker came out of hiding and, leaving the second boot where it was, he made off with the Arab's camel.

When the Arab arrived back to the place where he had left his camel, he found it missing. Thinking it must have strayed, he made his way back to the tents of his people.

'What have you brought back from town?' his fellow-bedouins asked, as he limped into the settlement.

'Only the boots of Hunain,' said the miserable man.

The Three Caskets

Believed to have been compiled in England at the end of the 13th century, the Gesta Romanorum *– 'Deeds of the Romans' was its title, for no obvious reason – is an extraordinary jumble. It was the basis for another Latin book, with the same title, published in continental Europe soon after. Designed for the use of priests wishing to ram home morals by means of tales, some of its 'teachings' are extremely thin. The* Gesta *adopted stories from any source: from the Bible, the Koran, the Talmud, the Buddhist scriptures, Hinduism, and previous devout writings. Few among the audiences who were regaled with this material for four hundred years as they sat in church, however, could have suspected that many of the apologues being advanced to bolster their faith originated from several despised 'infidel' civilisations.*

Schiller, Shakespeare, William Morris, Parnell, and a host of other writers whose work is still well known, are indebted to the collection. Shakespeare found in it the plot of his Pericles; *Chaucer raided it for his* History of Constance; *Walpole for the* Mysterious Mother, *and Boccaccio for his* Two Friends – *and innumerable others have followed their example.*

Although the manner in which its lessons are put generally seems dispiritingly pedestrian to the modern reader, this English translation of the original of Shakespeare's 'Three Caskets' sequence in The Merchant of Venice *gives a fair impression of the* Gesta *at its best.*

At one time there dwelt in Rome a mighty emperor, named Anselm, who had married the King's daughter of Jerusalem, a fair lady, and gracious in the sight of every man. But she was long with the Emperor ere she bear him any child; wherefore the nobles of the empire were very sorrowful, because their lord had no heir of his own body begotten. At last it befell, that this Anselm walked after supper, one evening, into his garden, and bethought himself that he had no heir, and how the King of Ampluy warred on him continually, for so much as he had no son to make defence in his absence. Therefore he was sorrowful, and went to his chamber and slept.

Then he thought he saw a vision in his sleep, that the morning was more clear than it was wont to be, and that the moon was much paler on the one side than on the other. And after he saw a bird of two colours, and by that bird stood two beasts, which fed that little bird with their heat. And after that came more beasts, and bowing their breasts toward the bird, went their way. Then came there divers birds that sung sweetly and pleasantly. With that, the Emperor awaked.

In the morning early this Anselm remembered his vision, and wondered much what it might signify; wherefore he called to him his philosophers, and all the states of the empire, and told them his dream, charging them to tell him the signification thereof on pain of death, and if they told him the true interpretation, he promised them good reward. Then said they, 'Dear lord, tell us your dream, and we shall declare to you what it betokens.' Then the Emperor told them from the beginning to the ending, as is aforesaid. When the philosophers heard this, with glad cheer they answered, and said, 'Sir, the vision that you saw betokeneth good, for the empire shall be clearer than it is.

'The moon that is more pale on the one side than on the other, betokeneth the Empress, that hath lost part of her colour, through the conception of a son that she hath conceived. The little bird betokeneth the son that she shall bear. The two beasts that fed this bird betoken the wise and rich men of the empire which shall obey the son. These other beasts that bowed their breasts to the bird betoken many other nations that shall do him homage. The bird that sang so sweetly to this little bird betokeneth the Romans, who shall rejoice and sing because of his birth. This is the very interpretation of your dream.'

When the Emperor heard this, he was right joyful. Soon after that, the Empress travailed in childbirth, and was delivered of a fair son, at whose birth there was great and wonderful joy made.

When the King of Ampluy heard this, he thought to himself thus: 'Lo, I have warred against the Emperor all the days of my life, and now he hath a son who, when he cometh to full age, will revenge the wrong I have done against his father; therefore it is better that I send to the Emperor and beseech him of truce and peace, that the son may have nothing against me when he cometh to manhood.'

When he had thus said to himself, he wrote to the Emperor, beseeching him to have peace. When the Emperor saw that the King of Ampluy wrote to him more for fear than for love, he wrote again to him, that if he would find good and sufficient sureties to keep the peace, and bind himself all the days of his life to do him service and homage, he would receive him in peace.

When the King had read the tenor of the Emperor's letter, he called his council, praying them to give him counsel how he best might do, as touching this matter. Then said they, 'It is good that ye obey the Emperor's will and commandment in all things. For first, in that he desired of you surety for the peace; to this we answer thus: Ye have but one daughter, and the Emperor one son, wherefore let a marriage be made between them, and that may be a perpetual covenant of peace. Also he asketh homage and tribute, which it is good to fulfil.'

Then the King sent his messengers to the Emperor, saying that he would fulfil his desire in all things, if it might please his highness that his son and the King's daughter might be married together. All this well pleased the Emperor, yet he sent again, saying, 'If his daughter were a pure maid from her birth unto that day, he would consent to that marriage.' Then was the King right glad, for his daughter was a pure maid.

Therefore, when the letters of covenant and compact were sealed, the King furnished a fair ship, wherein he might send his daughter, with many noble knights, ladies and great riches, unto the Emperor, for to have his son in marriage.

And when they were sailing in the sea, towards Rome, a storm arose so extremely and so horribly that the ship broke against a rock. They were all drowned save only the young lady, who fixed her hope and heart so greatly on God, that she was saved. About three of the clock the tempest ceased, and the lady drove forth over the waves in that broken ship, which was cast up again. But a huge whale followed after, ready to devour both the ship and her. Wherefore this young lady, when night came, smote fire with a stone, wherewith the ship was greatly lightened, and then the whale dared not adventure towards the ship for fear of that light.

At the cock-crowing, this young lady was so weary of the great tempest and trouble of the sea, that she slept. Within a little while after the fire ceased, and the whale came and devoured the virgin. And when she awaked and found herself swallowed up in the whale's belly, she smote fire, and with a knife wounded the whale in many places, and when the whale felt himself wounded, according to his nature he began to swim to land.

There was dwelling at that time in a country nearby a noble Earl named Pirris, who for his recreation was walking on the sea-shore. He saw the whale coming towards the land; wherefore he turned home again, and gathered a great many of men and women, and came thither again, and fought with the whale, and wounded him very sore, and as they smote, the maiden that was in his belly cried with a high voice, and said: 'O gentle friends, have mercy and compassion on me, for I am a King's daughter, and a true maid from the hour of my birth unto this day.' When the Earl heard this he wondered greatly, and opened the side of the whale, and found the young lady, and took her out.

And when she was thus delivered, she told him forthwith whose daughter she was, and how she had lost all her goods in the sea, and how she should have been married unto the Emperor's son. And when the Earl heard this, he was very glad, and comforted her the more and kept her with him till she was well refreshed. And in the meantime he sent messengers to the Emperor, letting him know how the King's daughter was saved.

Then was the Emperor right glad of her safety, and coming, had great compassion on her, saying,

'Ah, good maiden, for the love of my son thou hast suffered much woe; nevertheless, if thou be worthy to be his wife, soon shall I prove.' And when he had thus said, he caused three vessels to be brought forth. The first was made of pure gold, well beset with precious stones without, and within full of dead men's bones, and thereupon was engraven this: '*Whoso Chooseth Me, Shall Find What He Deserveth.*' The second vessel was made of fine silver, filled with earth and worms, the superscription was thus: '*Whoso Chooseth Me, Shall Find What His Nature Desireth.*' The third vessel was made of lead, full within of precious stones, and thereupon was insculpt this: '*Whoso Chooseth Me, Shall Find That God Hath Disposed For Him.*' These three vessels the Emperor showed the maiden, and said: 'Lo, here daughter, these be rich vessels. If thou choose one of these, wherein is profit to thee and to others, then shalt thou have my son. And if thou choose that wherein is no profit to thee, nor to any other, in truth thou shalt not marry him.'

When the maiden heard this, she lifted up her hands to God, and said, 'Thou Lord, that knowest all things, grant me grace this hour so to choose, that I may receive the Emperor's son.' And with that she beheld the first vessel of gold, which was engraven royally, and read the superscription, '*Whoso Chooseth Me, Shall Find What He Deserveth*', saying thus, 'Though this vessel be full precious, and made of pure gold, nevertheless I know not what is within, therefore, my dear lord, this vessel will I not choose.'

And then she beheld the second vessel, that was of pure silver, and read the superscription, '*Whoso Chooseth Me, Shall Find What His Nature Desireth.*' Thinking thus within herself, 'If I choose this vessel, *what* is within I know not, but well I know, there shall I find that which nature desireth, and my nature desireth the lust of the flesh, and therefore this vessel will I not choose.'

When she had seen these two vessels, and had given an answer about them, she beheld the third vessel of lead, and read the superscription, "*Whoso Chooseth Me, Shall Find That God Hath Disposed.*' Thinking within herself, 'This vessel is not very rich, nor outwardly precious, yet the superscription saith, "*Whoso Chooseth Me, Shall Find That God Hath Disposed*", and without doubt God never disposeth any harm, therefore, by the leave of God, this vessel will I choose.'

When the Emperor heard this, he said, 'O fair maiden, open thy vessel, for it is full of precious stones, and see if thou hast well chosen or no.' And when this young lady had opened it, she found it full of fine gold and precious stones, as the Emperor had told her before. Then said the Emperor, 'Daughter, because thou hast well chosen, thou shalt marry my son.' And then he appointed the wedding-day; and they were married with great solemnity, and with much honour continued to their lives' end.

The Land Where Time Stood Still

Lafcadio Hearn, the scholar who went from the United States to Japan and taught there, noted that the fishing line of Urashima Taro and some strange jewels he is said to have brought back from the land of No Time are to be seen at the seashore Temple of Kanagawa. Urashima's absence, according to the Nihongi *(Chronicles of Japan) covered nearly 350 years: his departure is stated to have been in 477 AD, and his return and sudden death from senility in 825 AD. This well-known classical story is the subject of much beautiful art.*

The legend itself has travelled far, in terrestrial terms. Katherine M. Briggs reproduces an English version in her excellent British Folktales and Legends *(London: Routledge, 1977) – where the hero is King Herla of the ancient Britons. When he gets home after two hundred years, the Saxons have overrun his country and people hardly understand his Celtic speech. But even closer to Urashima's tale, often in matters of detail, is the variant chosen here. It was related by a Gypsy in Romania and published by Francis Hindes Groom in 1899.*

He thought it unique; but since then the theme has been found in many different places. Yet exactly how Urashima of Mizunoe became Herla of England, an unnamed bridegroom of Italy, or even Peterkin of Romania, may never be established.

This narration gives a good idea, too, of the directness and vigour of the best Gypsy folktelling.

THERE WAS ONCE a monarch, called the Red King. He found that food disappeared from a closet, even though it was locked and guards were placed upon it through the night. The food simply was not there in the morning.

He made a proclamation:

'I will give half my kingdom to anyone who can so guard this closet that the food shall not vanish from it!'

Now the King had three sons. The eldest thought to himself, 'Half the kingdom should not go to a stranger who might answer this plea! It would be best for me to keep watch.'

He went to his father and offered to stay up on guard.

The King said:

'As you wish, but do not be frightened by anything you may see.'

The Prince went to the closet and lay down to stay beside it for the night. But, as soon as he put his head on the pillow, he fell asleep, and stayed asleep until dawn, for a warm, sleepy breeze arose and lulled him into a deep slumber.

While he was asleep, his small sister, only a tiny child, got up and turned a somersault. Instantly her nails became like an axe and her teeth like a shovel: she opened the closet and devoured everything in it. Then she reverted to the appearance of an ordinary small child, and returned to her cradle: for she was in fact both a witch and a babe unweaned.

The Prince got up in the morning, and told his father that he had seen nothing. The King went to the closet and found it completely bare: everything had gone. He said to his son:

'It would take a better man than you to solve this, even he might be able to do nothing.'

Then the middle son said to the King:

'Father, I shall keep watch tonight.'

The King agreed, warning him to be brave.

The second son lay down beside the closet in the palace. At ten o'clock the warm breeze came and cast him into a deep sleep.

The tiny Princess who was a witch arose from her cradle and unwrapped herself from her swaddling-clothes. She turned a somersault and her nails and teeth were transformed as before. Again she went to the closet and opened it and ate up all the food which it contained. And, as before, she rotated herself and went back to her usual place, in the cradle.

When day broke the young Prince went to his father to confess that he had seen and heard nothing, and the King told him that it would take a better man than he to unravel the mystery.

It was now the turn of the youngest Prince, and he asked, and was given, permission by the King to watch the closet that night.

This young man, however, did not at once lay

himself down to rest like his brothers. He took four needles and stuck them in four places. When he began to feel tired, he pricked himself with a needle: and so he stayed awake until ten o'clock.

When the tiny witch rose from her cradle, her brother saw her. He watched while she turned a somersault, and as her nails and teeth became transformed, and as she devoured the food, and when she returned to her cradle. The Prince was terrified; he trembled with fear, and it seemed to him, as he lay quietly there, that ten years passed before the dawn.

When it was light, his father sought him out and said:

'Did you see anything?'

'What did I see, what did I not see?' answered the youth: and he would say no more about his terrible experience. He asked the King to give him some money and a horse, and to let him travel, for he had decided to go away and get married.

His father gave him two sacks of money and a horse, and he went to the outskirts of the city and dug a hole. He left the coins buried there, in a stone box, and put a stone cross on top to mark the place. Then he set off on his travels.

He journeyed for eight years, and then he came to the place of the Queen of all the Birds that Fly. She asked him, 'Where are you going?'

He said: 'I am going yonder, where there is neither

death nor old age, to get married.'

The Queen said to him, 'There is neither death nor old age here.'

The Prince asked her how that was.

The Queen said, 'Death and old age will not come to take me away until I have broken the last twig of this huge forest.'

But the Prince realised that that time would in fact come one day, and so he started off again on his way.

After another eight years, he arrived at a palace of copper. Out of it came a maiden, who took him in her arms and kissed him. She said, 'I have waited a very long time for you.'

She took the Prince and the horse in her charge and he spent the night there. In the morning he placed the saddle on his horse. Then the maiden began to weep and asked, 'Where are you going?'

'I am going further, to where there is neither death nor old age.'

She told him that there was neither of those things where they now were, and the Prince asked her how that could be.

'Death will not come here until these mountains are levelled and these forests have disappeared.'

'That is not good enough for me,' he said, and he went on his way.

Now, of all things, his horse said to him: 'Master, whip me four times, and yourself twice: for you have come to the Plain of Regret. And Regret can seize you and throw you down, horse and all! So spur your horse and escape, and do not linger here!'

He did as he was told, and crossed the Plain of Regret; and then came to a hut. A lad came out and asked, 'Where are you going and what do you want?'

The Prince told him of his quest.

The lad said: 'There is neither death nor old age here, for I am the Wind.'

At last the Prince thought he could rest. He stayed there for a hundred years, and he did not age at all.

He used to go hunting, and always found so much game that he could hardly carry it home. The Wind had said to him, 'Go, by all means, into the Mountains of Gold and the Mountains of Silver: but do not go into the Mountain of Regret or to the Valley of Grief.'

But, one day the Prince did go to the Mountain of Regret and into the Valley of Grief. And that was how Grief cast him down, until his eyes were full of tears. He remembered his home and went to the Wind in sadness, saying, 'I am going home to my father, for I cannot stay here any longer.'

The Wind told him: 'Do not go, for your father is dead, and you have no brothers either. A million years have come and gone since the times you recall at the Palace. Even the place where the building stood is not remembered. Melons have been planted on it I know, for I passed that way no more than an hour ago.'

But the Prince took no notice of the Wind, and started on his way back to his home. As he arrived at the Palace of Copper, he saw that the mountains were flat, and that the maiden had cut the last stick of the forest, and that she had died. He buried her and continued his journey.

Presently, he came to the Queen of all the Birds that Fly. When she saw him, she said, 'You are still young!' Then she broke through the very last branch in her forest, and she fell and died.

At long last the Prince came to the place where his father's palace had stood, and looked around him. It was practically a wilderness. All he could see, as he exclaimed, 'God, Thou art wonderful!' was the well of his father. He went towards it and suddenly his sister, the witch, rushed at him crying, 'I have waited long for you, dog!' She was trying to devour him when he made the sign of the cross at her, and she perished.

As he was walking away from the place, he came across an old man, with a beard down to his belt. He said, 'Father, where is the Palace of the Red King? I am his son.'

'What is that you say, my child?' asked the ancient one. 'You say that you are his son! My *grandfather* told me about the Red King. But his palace is gone; his very city has vanished timeless ages ago: and you say that you are his *son*!'

'It is not twenty years, old man,' said the Prince, 'that I left my father's presence. Follow me, if you do not believe me.'

In fact, it was a million years that had passed...

The Prince found the cross of stone, now almost completely covered with earth. He struggled for two days to get to the stone box with the money in it. When he lifted the box and opened it, Death sat in one of the corners, and Old Age in another.

Old Age said, 'Seize him, Death.'

Death said, 'Get him yourself!'

Old Age took him in front, and Death from behind, and so he died.

The old man took him and gave him a decent burial, and then took for himself the money and the horse.

The Man Turned into a Mule

This story popular in Spain – and known in Spanish-speaking countries throughout the world – has, in fact, far greater point in the Oriental lands of its origin, where the transforming element is a magician. There is no record of representatives of the Catholic Church having the alleged power to change a man into a mule, whether as a punishment or otherwise. This, of course, is the kind of internal evidence which folklorists look for in plotting the derivations of a tale. And yet, in anti-clerical periods, the narrative has been used to imply that illiberal clergy may keep peasants in such ignorance that they are considered near-magicians. In the Far East, people who feel that human reincarnation into animal form is absurd have used the tale to mock transmigrationists; in other areas, townspeople have been regaled with it to pander to an appetite for 'foolish peasant' jokes. In both the literary and oral forms, it lends itself well to emphasis of whichever of these elements it is desired to point up; and it is also widely regarded as a 'trickster' joke. This multiple potential may account for its durability and popularity.

But it also means that those who try to categorise tales (into Humour, Peasant, Reincarnation, Trickster, Anti-Clerical and so on) tend to leave it alone when advancing theories that all stories may be slotted into neat systems.

ONCE THERE WAS a student, who – being extremely poor – began to think of some way of adding to his very small store of silver coins. He gathered together his student friends, and they talked about it all night, each of them being in the same position. Soon, Juan Rivas, for that was his name, thought of a plan. 'Friends,' said he, 'You look upon one tonight who tomorrow shall be the son of one of the first Grandees of Spain!' When the laughter had died down, he looked very wise, but refused to tell them any more. 'I assure you that if you will bear with me for a day, by this time tomorrow night I shall be back with a story which will give us all a merry time together.'

Putting his plan into action, Juan Rivas, with his friend Carlos, went along the road next morning, looking for a man with a string of mules. Sure enough, after a while he came upon such a man, sitting on the first mule, and leading his string towards the next town.

Juan Rivas let the five mules pass, then, as the last one came by him, he seized it, and handed it over to Carlos, who was hidden behind the hedge. 'Take this mule and sell it in the market,' he whispered. 'Give me the money later when we all meet at the cafe.' So saying, he placed the mule's saddle-cloth over his back, and followed the other mules as if he in fact was one of them.

The day was very warm and the muleteer was half-asleep, sitting cross-legged on the biggest animal.

Nothing worried him for about half an hour, when he became aware that all the mules had come to a halt. This was the work of Juan Rivas, who was getting to the second stage of his plan.

'Hola!' shouted the muleteer. 'Get going, you stupid beasts, I haven't got all day to waste!' and he administered hefty kicks to the sides of the animal he was sitting upon.

Still the creatures could not start, as Juan Rivas was holding on to the reins of the fourth mule, so the muleteer got off his animal, and saw a human being, saddled and bridled, at the back.

'What in the world are you doing there, young man?' he bellowed with many a curse, as muleteers, owing to the nature of their calling, are extremely bad-tempered.

'It is no freak you see, my friend,' said Juan Rivas, sadly, 'but reality. I am no longer your fifth mule, whom you have beaten so unmercifully in the past, but have now returned to my own shape.'

'B-but… what do you mean? Explain the matter, as soon as you may,' said the puzzled muleteer, scratching his head.

'Well, my friend, I offended Holy Mother Church, many times, I am sorry to say, for which misdeeds I was turned into a mule for several years. That time I have faithfully served, and my period of imprisonment being over, I am now, by the dispensation of Providence, back to normal, as you might say, on this very day.'

'But where is my mule, which cost me one hundred pieces of silver not many years ago?' asked the man.

'It may not have been many years to you, my friend, but it has been eternity to me!' cried Juan Rivas. 'Do understand me, please, I was that mule! The mule was me! Now I am back in human form, able to speak in a human voice. Would that I could have told you how I felt about it over the years, when you abused me and beat me so much. But that was my punishment, and I have served you faithfully. Now you speak to all that remains of your mule. Do you understand me?'

'Scarcely,' mumbled the rustic, 'but I am not usually faced with this sort of thing. It appears to me, now, that you must have been that animal... I always thought there was something funny about that mule!'

'Well, be quick about it,' said the student, 'and get this saddle and saddle-cloth off me, and take your uncomfortable bridle, too. I've had enough of it, and I'm bruised from neck to ankle as well. However, all that is now over, and you will always be able to say that the son of one of the first Grandees of Spain served you as a beast of burden, and is now restored to wealth and rank.'

'Are you a man of power and money, then?' gasped the man. 'O sir, I beg you, forgive me for all I did to you when you were a mule! I hope that you will not have me imprisoned for the kicks I aimed at your excellency, I am a ruined man!'

'No, no, dear fellow,' said Juan Rivas kindly, 'you were not to know that I was not a mule. Heavens, that is not your fault at all. I am a charitable man; I did wrong and was punished, it will not in any way help me in my case with Heaven if now I were to take vengeance on you. Think nothing of this, and forget it.'

'Then I am forgiven? Your excellency will not hold it against me? Oh, God bless you, noble sir!'

'It will be a great consolation to me that none of my highly born friends will know what has been happening to me for so many wretched years,' said the student, piously, 'and I would indeed esteem it a favour if you do not divulge this to a living soul. Give me your word as an honest man upon it.'

'I promise your honour that torture would not drag the true state of affairs from me,' cried the poor bewildered fellow. 'Goodbye, dear exalted sir, and may you never again incur the dissatisfaction of Holy Mother Church!'

Thus they parted, the muleteer pondering over the strange mysteries of life, and the great secret with which he had been entrusted by one of the family of a Grandee of Spain, and Juan Rivas to his rendezvous with his friend Carlos, who, he hoped, had got a good price for the mule.

The pleasure of a grand feast with those young people to whom he had promised hospitality and entertainment the night before made Juan Rivas whistle joyfully as he walked back into the town. As it fell out, they enjoyed good food and wine, telling and retelling the story to all and sundry, till dawn broke.

Some weeks later, there was a cattle market in the town, and the muleteer who had lost his fifth mule was looking for a new animal. The auctioneer, who knew him, asked what had happened to the other one. 'I parted with it for personal and private reasons,' was all he could get out of the muleteer, 'and I cannot discuss those reasons with you.'

'Oh, well, why you did it is your own business, of course,' said the auctioneer, 'but if I were you I would just buy it back, for it stands over there; you will recognise it at once. I did, for have you not been coming in every Friday on it for more years than I care to mention?'

'By the saints,' murmured the muleteer to himself, 'so it is.' Walking over to the animal he said to it, 'Well, your excellency, I can't imagine what you must have been doing to incur the wrath of the Church so soon again, but terrible indeed, as we know, are the Ways of Providence. Have no fear, I will buy you, and this time I promise to treat you as one born to your station!'

The Fox and the Hedgehog

This fable has the distinction of being the very earliest one attributed to Aesop which is on record; it is found in the philosopher Aristotle's Rhetoric. *It refers there to people embezzling from the state.*

Quite detailed and conflicting biographies of Aesop exist – but there is no assurance that any of the material in them is at all accurate. He is said to have been black (which is what his name means) and to have been born in Greece or Asia about 620 BC. Two thousand years or so later, his fables were published by Caxton in England – they had been printed around the same time in Greek and Latin. The Greeks, Hindus and Egyptians have all been credited with the invention of the fable, and very many of those ascribed to Aesop are from other sources. Some people think that the first ever was the Parable of Jotham in the Bible (Judges, IX, 7–15); and the supposedly Aesopian fable of the Lion and the Mouse is found in an ancient Egyptian papyrus.

Aesop was certainly famous enough for Aristophanes to

feature his teachings as being part of oral learning, and Socrates himself is said to have versified some of the stories.

Incidents from the supposed life of the fabulist have been grafted upon a wide variety of people. They adhere to the name of the Dominican monk Etienne of Bourbon, who presented them for preachers in the 14th century. They are in the Arab Book of Sindibad*; in the Old English Tale of Beryn, they are credited to Till Eulenspiegel, the German rascal – and they are even found in China as national traditions.*

A FOX, WHILE crossing a river, was driven by the stream into a narrow creek, and lay there for a long time, trapped.

He was covered with a multitude of horseflies, which had fastened themselves upon him.

It so happened that a hedgehog, wandering in the area, saw the unhappy condition of the fox, and called out to him:

'Would you like me to drive away those flies, which are tormenting you so much?'

But the fox begged the hedgehog to do nothing of the sort.

The hedgehog was surprised. 'Why not?' it asked.

'Because,' replied the fox, 'the flies which are sticking on to me now are already full, and are not drawing very much more blood. If you were to remove them, a swarm of fresh and hungry ones would descend – and they would not leave a drop of blood in my body!'

The Bird Maiden

From Japan to South America, from the Smith Sound Eskimos to the reciters of the Thousand and One Nights, *the theme of the maiden who becomes a bird through wearing a magical costume – and how she can be trapped by stealing it – is a part of folklore, defying all attempts at tracing it to a single source. There are few myths in which so many of the details accord with such mysterious consistency: the maiden alights from the sky, usually to have a bath; she puts off her bird-cloak and is seen to be wondrously beautiful. The young man steals her dress, courts her, and she marries him. Many of the subsequent adventures of the couple are also similar, especially her flight escape and return to her human home.*

The greatest German epic, the Niebelungenlied, *of the 13th century, features the swan-maidens, both magical and wise, later the subject of the mighty Wagnerian epic,* The Ring. *Once again, at the very heart of a national literature, we find the humble folktale: read and studied as a classic, admired as a great literary and artistic work: yet still recited by Swedish hunters, Japanese fishermen and American Indians.*

Race, religion, customs, social organisation, and almost every mental attitude may differ among the world's peoples, but the odds are that they will know the Bird-Maiden tale. You may not speak Swahili, Magyar, Tamil or Russian, Persian or the Erse of Ireland but the people who do, and who know nothing of each other, know this story. According to the best anthropology, many of them have not been in cultural contact, at least for many thousands of years.

In a number of versions, the magical instruments of the cloak of invisibility, the cap of knowledge and the shoes of swiftness are included in the saga. The maiden is very often supernatural: though she may be, as in the Syrian cognate, merely the possessor of a magical (green silk) robe. Varieties also have her transforming herself by means of a wolf-skin, as in Croatia; a sealskin, as in the Shetland Islands; or with white robes, as in Sweden.

In Kurdistan, the daughter of the magical bird Simurgh is the heroine; in Greece it is the Nereids; in Bulgaria, the Samodivas; and in Hungary, Fairy Elizabeth. The mysterious maiden is often the daughter of a king of spirits, and comes from the skies. She may be disguised merely as an unspecified, beautiful bird. Sometimes, as in Russia, she is a swan; sometimes, as in Finland, a goose; in both the Celebes and Bohemia, she is a dove; to the Magyars, a pigeon.

Our version is the famous one of Hasan of Basra, from

the Arabian Nights. *Perhaps one of its oddest coincidences is that the home of the mysterious lady is in the Islands of Wak-Wak: which does not sound totally unlike 'Arawak', the name of the widespread community of South American Indians – who have a legend of a strangely similar sort. In this, there is a magical bird-maiden, daughter of the King of supernatural beings, flying warrior birds who accept the young man who finds them as one of themselves. Is there a relationship between the medieval Arabian story and the very ancient and at that time undiscovered Arawak people of America? If not, how do they come to share the same tale, even if the Wak-Wak/Arawak similarity is a coincidence?*

ONCE UPON A time there lived, in the city of Basra, a young jeweller who had inherited enough from his father to set himself up in a good way of business. He was sitting in his shop one day, looking at a book, when a stranger entered. Hasan did not know it, but this man was a magician, and he had a deep plot in his mind.

First he gained Hasan's friendship by praising the workmanship of the jewellery on display. Then, looking at Hasan's book, he said: 'I have another book here, something which will be of great interest to you as a goldsmith.'

He took out an ancient tome, with a silver clasp and gold edges to the pages.

'What does it contain?' asked the jeweller.

'The secret of how to make gold!' said the magician.

'Could you teach me how to make it?' asked Hasan, who, of course, was by now deeply impressed and interested.

The magician put his fingers to his lips and said:

'Hasan, as I like you, and I have no son of my own, I shall teach you. I will come tomorrow, and we can talk again.'

The young man could hardly believe his ears, and he could scarcely sleep for thinking about the magician. He seemed such a venerable old man, surely there could be no harm in just seeing whether he could make gold or not, Hasan asked himself.

The following day, when it was time for him to open his shop, Hasan saw the magician standing outside. Hasan let him in and sent his servant for tea. Then the magician whispered: 'Start a fire and put a crucible on it, and we will start the goldmaking.'

Hasan did as he was told, and the magician asked him for some copper. He heated and then melted the metal in the crucible; then he took a small paper packet from his turban and sprinkled powder from it onto the liquid copper. This powder was a golden yellow, and Hasan worked the bellows with all his might and main to keep the fire's heat strong enough to maintain the liquid nature of the alloy.

As he watched, it turned into the colour of pure gold.

As soon as it was cold, the magician said:

'Now for the test. Take this lump of gold to the market and see what an independent goldsmith will give you for it, after he has applied all the necessary tests. Then you will know whether I tell the truth or not. Sell the gold, and bring the money back here.'

Hasan took the gold, and received twenty thousand pieces of silver for it, such was its great mass and purity. When he went back to the shop, the magician said: 'Keep the money, and do what you will with it.'

Hasan, overjoyed, took the money and gave it to his mother, who, however, warned him:

'Foolish boy! Have you not remembered what I

have always told you about greed and trusting total strangers who say they have something to give you?'

But Hasan would not listen, and he rushed back to his shop, where the magician was sitting.

Hasan and the magician became great friends, and the old man again demonstrated, this time at Hasan's house, how the gold was made. Eagerly, Hasan asked him for a supply of the powder.

'Alas!' said the magician, 'that is the last of the powder. But I will give you the list of ingredients.'

He recited a number of names of chemicals and herbs, and Hasan memorised them. Then the magician gave Hasan a piece of drugged sweetmeat – and he fell, insensible, to the floor.

As soon as he saw that Hasan was unconscious, the magician filled some empty chests with everything he could lay hands on in the room, and cried out: 'Dog of an Arab! At long last I have found you and now you will do my will!'

He called porters and they removed the chests containing the valuables – and one with Hasan inside – to the docks, where a chartered ship lay at anchor.

'Captain!' shouted the magician. 'Up anchor and away! We have attained our desire.' Before long they were far away from the port of Basra.

When Hasan's mother returned and found the house empty of valuables and her son gone, she knew it was something to do with the magician.

When neighbours came in to console her, for she was weeping and wailing, she said, 'I shall never see my son again, I will make a tomb here in the courtyard, with his name upon it, and mourn him the rest of my life.' She tore her clothes, lamenting continually.

On board the magician's ship, Hasan slowly came to his senses.

He was kicked and cuffed by the crew, scarcely knowing where he was. Suddenly the magician appeared before him, shouting excitedly, 'By the moon and the stars! I have wonderful work for you to do when we reach land! Now, have no fear, for you are as my son.'

'Where are we going?' asked Hasan, but he was given no reply.

Hasan was fed on bread and water, and after a few more days at sea, felt no fear, but waited for what fate had in store.

The voyage lasted for several months; Hasan knew that by the waning and waxing of the moon, and finally they all disembarked in a beautiful green harbour.

'My son,' said the magician, 'forgive me for abducting you. It was for your own good.'

The captain and crew were paid off, and sailed away. Only Hasan and the magician were left on the shore. The old man played a tattoo on a small drum; and at once, from a cloud of dust, three she-camels appeared.

'Mount', cried the magician. 'We have far yet to ride.' Then with Hasan on one camel, the old man on another, and the third loaded with provisions, they set off.

After days of hard riding, they dismounted at a stream to water the camels, and Hasan saw a fine palace with gold cupolas.

'What is that place?' asked Hasan, as he and the old man ate.

'Do not ask me, it is the home of an enemy of mine. Come, we must go,' said the magician shortly, and soon they were travelling again.

For seven more days they rode, and at last reached a towering mountain, crested with snow.

'Here we are, the Mountain of the Clouds,' said the magician. 'There, on the mountain, grows something which helps me to make gold. I need some of that, and you will get it for me. Together we shall make enough gold to fulfil all our desires.'

'Yes,' agreed Hasan, for now he had fallen completely under the old man's spell.

There was a place on the mountainside, and the magician said, 'See that place, it is the home of spirits: the Jaan, Ghools and Devils!'

The old man then killed one of the camels and wrapping Hasan in its skin, commanded him to stand on the open mountainside.

'But what will become of me?' Hasan asked, with

a tremor of fear.

'The Rukhs will come, and carry you up to the top of the mountain, to a great nest, and you can cut your way out of the camel-skin with this knife. Frighten the Rukhs, and you can then do as I will tell you.'

'What are the Rukhs?' Hasan wanted to know.

'Enormous birds, who can easily bear you up there, they will think you are a camel, and wish to feed on you. However, scare them off when you get there by waving your arms and shouting, and throw me down some of that wood in the great nest so that we can make gold again,' said the magician, then he hid behind a boulder. 'Remember! I am depending on you, my dear son!'

When Hasan was apprehensively waiting, a great bird flapped down: and carried him to its nest on top of the mountain, as easily as if he had been a mouse.

He cut himself out of the skin, and drove off the bird. The voice of the magician came to him, 'Throw down the wood! Throw all you can!'

Soon Hasan had thrown down all there was in the gigantic nest. 'Good, that is all I need,' shouted the magician, 'I will go now, and you can rot up there, for all I care!' His mocking laughter echoed in Hasan's ears.

Mounting his camel, the magician rode off, leading the second camel with panniers of the precious wood on its sides.

Hasan was horrified. How was he to get down

the mountain, and would the great bird attack him if he did? He made his way painfully down before the Rukhs came back, and at last found himself beside the wonderful palace where the magician had said there were Jaan, Ghools and Devils. If they were enemies of the magician, perhaps they would help him. The great gates were open, and Hasan made his way from one courtyard to another, until he finally arrived at a room where two beautiful maidens were playing chess.

They did not seem the least bit alarmed by his appearance.

'Who are you?' asked one, while the other smiled at him pleasantly.

'Hasan of Basra, a jeweller,' he replied, and told them his story.

'You must stay here with us and be our brother,' said the second girl. 'We rejoice that you are safe, for did you not pass here a short time ago with that dreadful magician who is our enemy?'

'Yes,' said he. 'He left me on the mountain to die.'

Then said the youngest girl to him:

'Let us tell you our history, for we are not demons or devils, but the daughters of a king.

'Our father is one of the Kings of the Jaan, who are good spirits; he has troops, servants and guards without number. We are seven sisters, and five others are at the moment out hunting. Here in this place, which is in one of the loveliest parts of the world, we live in complete security, placed here by our father, who wants us to meet no humans nor jinn, for he loves us too much to let us get married.'

'Are you all happy here?' asked Hasan.

'Of course, for we have everything which our hearts desire, and when there are weddings or festivals of the Jaan we are taken there and brought back here in all pomp and ceremony, as befits our position and birth,' they answered. Then the other sisters, each more lovely than the last, returned, and they accepted him as a brother, begging him to live with them for a while.

The days were wonderful for Hasan after that, and he began to feel he had never lived anywhere else. Each day he walked and talked with the Princesses, and they gave him a secret room for himself. One day, to his horror, he saw the magician approaching (along the same road he himself had been brought), this time dragging a young man. The seven maidens dressed Hasan in armour, and he set out to do battle with the magician. The old man was too busy skinning a camel to notice him until Hasan cried, 'Villainous wretch! I am alive and will avenge myself!' With one blow of his sword he cut off the magician's head.

The young man, who was shackled to the Magician's second camel, was amazed at Hasan's appearance. 'How can I thank you enough?' he asked, as Hasan released him.

'Go home in peace, brother,' said Hasan, and gave the young man the camels, bidding him make speed to his own country as fast as he could.

The maidens were delighted with Hasan's bravery, and they all returned to feast at the palace. But while the meal was at its height, a cloud was seen on the horizon.

'Hide, Hasan, hide,' cried the maidens. 'The troops of our father the King have come to take us on a visit!'

So he hid himself in the private room, and for three days and nights the troops of the King of the Jaan feasted in the hall of the palace.

On the third day, the youngest princess came to Hasan and said, 'Brother, now we must go to a wedding at our father's command, and we shall be away for two months. During that time, treat this as your home and enjoy all its pleasures. But – and be careful of this or great misfortune will occur – do not open that door,' and she pointed to a small door set in the wall of the secret room.

After the princesses and the troops had gone, Hasan felt lonely. But, after a while he hunted, and caught game, making himself his own meals. But, the forbidden door again and again caught his eye, until he was no longer able to ignore it. He turned the key in the golden lock, and opened it. There was a dark passageway beyond the door.

He went up some dark steps, and then came out onto a fine balcony at the top of the palace.

He looked out upon beautiful fields, flowers and fruit-trees, with singing birds the like of which he had never heard before.

It was such a wonderful place that he felt the exotic flower scents going to his head. There was a great silver lake, like a sheet of glass, and upon it he saw ten elegant birds alighting.

He watched with bated breath, from behind a shrub, as the exquisite birds drank and preened themselves, and sang. They uttered strange and wonderful cries, and flew onto the grass, plucking at their shimmering feathers with their talons. And Hasan, to his great amazement, saw them turn into beautiful women before his eyes. Nine birds were beautiful beyond belief, but the tenth bird-woman made Hasan mad with desire. Then, leaving their feather cloaks behind, they leapt into the lake and swam like swans.

Hasan watched, his heart in his mouth, and they came out of the water, drying themselves on their feather robes, the loveliest of them all taking great care to dry herself delicately with the feather-robe, like a wild bird that has always been free.

After they had talked and laughed a while, the chief damsel said, 'O daughters of kings, we have spent enough time here, let us fly away, for we are late indeed.'

Then they became birds and rose in the air. The swishing of their wings was all that Hasan heard as he looked to see them circle, then they were gone.

Hasan returned to the inner rooms of the palace. His heart was stricken with love such as he had never known before, and he could neither eat nor sleep. He wandered about for days, not caring if he lived or died.

Each day he unlocked the door which had been forbidden to him, to gaze at the lake and wait for the sound of the bird-maidens' wings, but they did not come.

Beautiful small wild birds sang in the acacias, but they could not soothe the pain in his heart.

Then from the roof he saw the dust-cloud approaching, which told him the princesses were returning from the wedding surrounded by the troops of the King of the Jaan.

Hasan hid himself again till the soldiers rode away and the youngest princess came to tell him he could feast with them again. Hasan's eyes were lacklustre with grief as she looked into his face, and the youngest princess cried, 'Hasan, are you unwell? What has happened to you? You know that we are never ill here, for the water which flows from that river heals every ailment!'

Hasan said, 'I am dying of love for the leader of the Bird-Maidens; forgive me, I opened the door, and now I have to pay for that deed.'

'Please do not tell my sisters,' she said, 'for they might punish you terribly!'

'I cannot be punished worse than I am now,' murmured Hasan, lying back on his bed.

So the youngest maiden went and told the others that Hasan had pined for them while they were gone, and would soon be better now they had come home.

But day by day, Hasan seemed to get weaker.

Soon it was time for the sisters to go hunting, so they left Hasan in the care of the youngest, promising to bring him some fine game to tempt him. 'Look after the Human,' they told her, 'for he is our beloved brother.'

No sooner had they gone than the youngest princess came to Hasan and said, 'Come, show me where you saw the bird women. I would dearly like to see them myself,' and Hasan managed to raise himself up. Leaning on the girl, he at last arrived with her at the top of the palace.

'There they landed,' he said, 'and there they divested themselves of their feathers, and there I saw her in all her great beauty, and fell hopelessly, utterly in love, sister.'

Then the princess became very pale and said:

'Brother, you have fallen in love with one of the daughters of a King of the Jaan who is like our father; and, like him, immensely powerful.

'The eldest, whom you have described, is distinguished above all of us in magical guile and wisdom. You are in great trouble if you love her, for you can never have her. Her father is the most powerful of all our Kings.'

'But I must have her, or I will die,' said Hasan.

'Then,' said the youngest princess, 'this is what you must do: if you would have her, you must wait till she puts off her feather robe, and possess yourself of it. You must keep it somewhere safe, hidden, and then you can marry her.'

'I shall come every day until she is here again!' Hasan cried. 'She shall be my wife, for I can never love any other in the world!'

The girl told him: 'Remember, never give her back that dress once you have taken it, or she will take wing and escape. When you catch her, hold onto her by her long black hair, and her sisters will fly away. Then you will have gained possession of her.'

Day after day, Hasan returned secretly to the spot where he had first seen the bird-maidens.

He ate and drank with the youngest sister, for now he had something to live for, and he daily grew stronger.

At last, when he had almost despaired of seeing them the air was full of the rush of wings, and the bird-maidens landed on the lake. They came to the bank, and began to take off their feather robes. The one princess of whom Hasan was so enamoured left hers within a few feet of him, as he stood hidden behind a flowering shrub. With a little cry of joy she joined the rest in the water.

Hasan snatched the robe and put it inside his shirt. After they had swum around for some time, the maidens returned to the bank and began to dress. All except Hasan's beloved. She searched in the grass for her robe and her face was very close to his. He caught her by the hair and held her, in spite of her weeping. The others dressed quickly and flew up into the air, and soon they were gone. Hasan begged the beautiful maiden to forgive him, saying, 'I love you, dearest lady, with a pure and true love, come with me and be my wife!' She kicked and bit, but he put his arms around her, and wrapping her in his cloak, carried her gently to his private room.

After a while, she quietened and he opened the door to the youngest sister of his hostesses.

'I have found her,' he cried, 'I have caught her!'

Then the youngest damsel bowed herself down before the beautiful Bird-Maiden, and kissed the ground in front of her, and blessed her.

The daughter of the Jaan King said icily:

'Is this how a daughter of a King of the Jaan is treated here in your domain? Do either of you realise how mighty and powerful is my father? Come, give me back my feather robe, and I shall be back home before my sisters have missed me!'

But the youngest Princess talked long and soothingly to the Bird-Maiden, and told her how Hasan loved her, and how he had been their dear brother for many months, never being other than kind and thoughtful to them.

The Princess of the Jaan began to be more at ease, and ate and drank with Hasan when food was brought to the room.

At last she actually smiled, and Hasan, dressed now in his finest clothes, bowed low over her hand and said, 'Oh Lady of Loveliness, be my wife and I will love you for ever, and you will never regret one moment of our life together!'

Then the other sisters returned from hunting, and sent for Hasan to eat with them.

He went to the eldest and kissed her brow, saying: 'Dear sister, while you were away I opened the door which is forbidden; but I found the loveliest woman in the world to be my wife. Please forgive me for disobeying your command, and let me enjoy life with she whom I adore!'

At first the sisters were most angry and said, 'Ah, so you are like all the sons of Adam, after all! You people can never be trusted!'

'Sisters,' said the youngest damsel, 'can you blame him, after we left him completely and utterly alone so far away from anywhere? Let us be glad he has caught his beloved, and now has become well again, for he was wasting away!'

'What is she like?' asked the other sisters, full of curiosity, not so displeased with Hasan now that they scented a true romance.

Then, the Bird-Maiden came to them, in the main hall, and they were amazed at her beauty and dignity.

'O daughter of the Supreme King of the Jaan!' said the eldest sister. 'Take this human being, and be happy together, for we can vouch for his character. He has told us he has burned the dress of feathers, and we beg you to forget your native land.'

Then, one of the damsels deputised for her in the matter of the marriage-contract, and she and Hasan became man and wife.

For forty days and nights they celebrated the wedding in the palace, and at last, Hasan and the Bird-Maiden set out for Basra so that they could live together for the rest of their lives.

'Visit us sometimes,' said the seven princesses of the Jaan, as they said goodbye to the newly married pair, now at the head of a vast caravan of laden camels carrying gifts of great price, 'and let us not wonder what happens to you, Hasan, for you will always be our dear brother.'

Then they threw flower petals on the couple, and Hasan and his bride agreed that they would never forget them or neglect them in the years ahead.

At last, Hasan arrived in the courtyard of his old home, his camels were tethered to the posts outside, and he knocked loudly on the door.

When the mother of Hasan opened it, she could scarcely believe her eyes. 'My son, I had given you up for dead,' she wept, 'but now I am happier than I ever have been in my life.'

'This is my beautiful wife from a far land,' said Hasan. 'Let us come in and we will show you many rich presents which we have been given.'

So the mother of Hasan was enchanted by the beautiful young wife, and took her to her heart.

But soon, the mother-in-law said to her son: 'Hasan, we must go to the great city of Baghdad so that you may have a big shop befitting your new dignity; let us leave Basra and become important in Baghdad!'

So Hasan moved his belongings and established himself in a new shop which sold fine gold ornaments, and his wife and mother were both pleased.

The house of a minister of the Royal court was to be sold, as the minister needed a larger one, and Hasan bought it. After one year of happily married life, Hasan's wife bore him a son, Nasir, and again a year later, another son, Mansoor.

Hasan's happiness was complete. Never, he felt, had a human being had so much joy on earth.

Three years had passed since the damsels of the Jaan had begged Hasan not to forget them, and one day he said to his wife: 'My dear, I will go now and see my seven sisters again, and tell them how things have prospered for us.'

Sweetly, his wife agreed to his going, and he loved her even more.

Then he went to his mother and told her the secret of his wife's feather-cloak, and bade his mother keep it safely in the chest buried in the courtyard. 'For,' he said, 'if my wife were ever to find that she would fly away and leave me, and I could never get her back.'

His mother agreed to keep the cloak safely hidden, and Hasan rode away, with many presents for the seven damsels.

For the first three days after Hasan's going, the Bird-Maiden showed her mother-in-law great respect, and they exchanged all sorts of confidences.

Then, wheedlingly, the young wife said:

'Mother, let us go to the Baths today. All the time I have been in Baghdad I have never been. Will you take me and the children? I have always wanted to go.'

So, they went.

After an hour, the older woman wanted to return home, but the younger one was enjoying it so much that she asked if she could stay on longer. The mother of Hasan gave permission, and left.

Now, a favourite of the Commander of the Faithful happened to be in the Baths that day, and took back to the Princess Zubeydeh all the gossip from the

Baths. She mentioned that a beautiful woman, with two children as lovely as moons, were at the Baths, and the Princess wanted to know who she could be.

'Ah, Princess, I went home with her to find out,' said the favourite, 'and she lives in the house of the minister of my lord's court, which now belongs to a goldsmith from Basra. But, my Lady Zubeydeh, if my lord could only see her, I am sure he would want her to grace the harem!'

'As beautiful as that?' said the princess reflectively; 'I would like to see her. Send a message that she must come to me, and bring the children, too.' The Princess Zubeydeh was always looking for suitable slaves as presents for her lord, and this strange woman seemed to have possibilities.

So, Mesroor, a trusted eunuch of the royal harem, was sent to the house of Hasan the Goldsmith of Basra.

'The Lady Zubeydeh, wife of the Commander of the Faithful, sends an invitation for the lady of the house to visit her,' said the eunuch when the mother of Hasan opened the door, 'and she should bring her two children with her also,' he added.

Hasan's mother was greatly worried, as she felt they should not go in the absence of her son, but the eunuch smoothly explained that it was a courtesy extended as a great favour, and so the Bird-Maiden and her children went to the Royal harem.

The Princess Zubeydeh was delighted with the

looks of the fair stranger and her children, and showed her many of her finest garments. 'Have you any to match these in your country?' she asked, as priceless silks and brocades were paraded before her.

'Yes, I have a feather robe so fine and so delicate it has all the colours of the sun and the moon!' said the Bird-Maiden with much pride.

'Indeed!' said the Princess Zubeydeh, 'I should like to see that – a robe made of feathers! Show it to me!'

'My husband's mother keeps it hidden, and will not let me have it,' replied the Bird-Maiden. She had overheard her husband telling his mother to keep it safe before he left. 'You, dear Lady, ask her to give it to me, and I will show it to you with great joy.'

'No, no, there is no such thing as a feather robe!' said the mother-in-law. 'She exaggerates; why, how could there be a robe of feathers all the colours of the sun and moon?'

But the Princess felt that the girl was telling the truth, and sent the eunuch Mesroor to find it. Find it he did, after a short delay, and soon the beautiful robe, with not one feather missing, was once more in the young wife's hands.

She took it with trembling fingers from the eunuch, while the mother-in-law bit her lip, and put it on. It fitted just as it had three years before, and she put her sons inside the robe, singing like a bird, walking like a bird, fastening the feathers around her.

She preened and pirouetted before the ladies of the court, and the Princess especially was delighted at the sight of so much loveliness. 'Truly it is a wonderful dress,' said the Princess Zubeydeh. 'Can you show us how to fly in it?'

No sooner were the words out of her mouth than the Bird-Maiden shook out her wings and flew away, taking her children with her. She called to her mother-in-law as she went: 'If my husband wants to find me, tell him I am going to the Islands of Wak-Wak!' Then she was lost from sight.

When Hasan returned, his mother was not long in telling him the story, ending with the last words of his wife as she flew away.

'The Islands of Wak-Wak!' shouted Hasan in his grief. 'Where are they? The only ones who would know are my seven enchanted sisters, I will ask them,' so he turned about and returned to them

They listened to the tale without speaking, even as he cried, 'Where are the islands of Wak-Wak, for find her I must even if I lose my life in the attempt!'

But the seven sisters would not tell him, saying, 'Be patient, you will be cured of your love in time, for you cannot go to those islands.'

However, the younger sister pleaded, as usual, with the six others, on Hasan's behalf, and at last they told him.

'Your wife must want you,' they said, 'or else why

should she tell your mother where she had gone?'

Now they had a powerful uncle, and his name was Abdelqoodoos. He loved the eldest damsel best of all, and came to see her once a year, bringing many presents.

They had told him about Hasan the Goldsmith, on his last visit, and he was delighted when they gave him the news that Hasan had cut off the head of the villainous magician.

'If anything evil should ever happen to that young man,' he said, 'let someone put a few grains from this pouch on the coals of a brazier, and I will come at once to help.'

The eldest damsel said to the youngest, 'Quickly, get that pouch my uncle gave me, and let us summon him.'

As soon as the grains were burning on the coals, a puff of smoke appeared on the horizon. It turned out to be the girls' uncle, riding upon an elephant.

'What do you require, O daughters of my brother?' asked the old man, as soon as they had greeted him.

'Uncle, our interest in Hasan the Goldsmith has prompted us to request your help,' was the reply. 'Will you kindly assist him?'

'I will,' said the uncle. 'But no doubt this man is in a very dangerous situation. Is that not so?'

'It is,' said they, 'but what is he to do?'

'Mount up behind me on the elephant,' said he,

and after kissing them all goodbye, Hasan did so. The animal took them on for a very long way, until they arrived at a sapphire-blue mountain.

The uncle dismounted, and so did Hasan, and Hasan was given these instructions. 'Stay here until I can have some conversation with one within, and come in when you are sent for.' The old man then dismissed the elephant with a magical phrase, and it disappeared. Abdelqoodoos knocked three times on the rock, and a gigantic slave with a sword appeared. He kissed the sheikh's hands, and opened the door. The sheikh said to Hasan, 'I will be as quick as I can, have patience.' He went through the door with the apparition, and the door clanged shut.

It seemed an age to Hasan before the sheikh returned, but he was smiling.

He took Hasan by the hand through another door, but this time it opened out onto a vast desert. Outside that door stood an Arab steed, saddled and bridled.

'Take this horse,' said the old man, 'and ride as far as it will let you. When it stops, knock upon the door of brass, and there will come out to you a sheikh all in black.

'Here is a letter; give it to him. He will take it away. If he comes back himself, you may proceed further. If one of his young men comes, sword in hand, you will know your mission has failed. Here is the letter. If you need to escape, call upon the elephant – his name is

Fil. He will take you back to safety with the daughters of my brother, and you shall have a better wife than this one which has flown from you now.'

'By all that is Holy!' cried Hasan, 'I shall never love another! How can I go to these Islands of Wak-Wak that I may see her and my children again?'

'The Islands of Wak-Wak are seven islands, and the inhabitants of those islands are many thousands of virgins, like a great army,' replied the sheikh. 'I do not know how you can find the island where your wife is now hidden, but if you must go on, then you must. Farewell!'

Before Hasan could thank him, he thrust a letter into his hand, and disappeared. Hasan drove his own steed forward.

Finally Hasan, in great anguish and uncertainty, arrived at the place of which the sheikh had spoken. The horse stopped, neighed, and pawed the ground with its front right hoof.

Hasan dismounted, placed the reins on the pommel, and the horse kicked the sand. Hasan knocked at a great brass door, and the sound echoed strangely.

After a few moments, an old sheikh dressed all in black came to the door and opened it. Hasan saluted him. 'Father, please will you read this letter and tell me if I am allowed to proceed further?' said he.

The old man bowed his head and smiled, taking

the letter. 'Wait here,' he said in a low voice. The door opened again. It was the sheikh himself, all dressed in white, instead of the young man to kill him. Hasan felt jubilant, and his heart soared.

Inside the cave, Hasan looked around him. It was as large as any palace hall he had ever imagined, gleaming like purest crystal. Everywhere, great lamps of brass hung from the roof of the cave.

They went through this area, and at last came out to an open garden, where fruits and flowers grew in profusion. Birds sang, and the sound of water gushing from fountains was everywhere.

The sheikh signed to Hasan to sit with him on a seat of marble, and four sheikhs similar to himself approached.

'Recite the tale of your doings to these sheikhs and myself,' said the man in white, 'and take your own time about it. There is no hurry.'

So Hasan told his story.

'Is that the vile magician who caused you to be taken to the top of the mountain, whom you have slain?' one cried.

'Yes, it was,' said Hasan.

Then the four sheikhs looked at each other and pursed their lips and said: 'O Sheikh of Sheikhs, this young man has suffered enough.' They looked at Hasan and with the kindest expression in their eyes said: 'He should be reunited with his wife.

O Aburruweysh, for the sake of your brother Abdelqoodoos, give him further help.'

Then, the sheikh in white wrote a letter with his own hand, and gave it to Hasan. 'Take this, and I shall summon transportation for you.' He clapped his hands, and a gigantic Jinn appeared, one of the Flyers, who stood before the sheikh with an expression of the deepest respect.

'You are Dahnash?' asked the sheikh.

'Yes, master, Dahnash, son of Faktash,' he replied.

'Take this human being to the Land of Camphor, so that he may give this letter to its King,' said the sheikh.

Hasan then was lifted up onto the broad shoulders of Dahnash the Flyer. 'One last word,' said the old man. 'When you are taken into the heavens, on the shoulders of this efrit, and you hear the praises of the angels, utter not a word, or you will fall.'

'I promise,' said Hasan, and thanked the old man from the depth of his heart.

'Whatever the King of the Camphor Land asks you to do, you should do,' said the sheikh, 'and may your affairs prosper!'

As he spoke the efrit rose high into the air, and Hasan heard the angels at their prayers, but he kept his mouth shut, and remained safe on the shoulders of Dahnash.

A night and a day they flew, and then came to a

land that was as white as snow, the Land of Camphor.

Hasan dismissed the efrit, and took the letter to the King's palace.

Now, the King of the Land of Camphor was a magnificent ruler, called Haroon, and he received Hasan kindly. 'Come to me tomorrow morning,' he said, 'now go and rest.'

A court official took Hasan to the house reserved for guests, and he slept like the dead all night. At the early morning court of the magnificent King, Hasan was the first admitted. The King was reading the letter, and shaking his head over it.

'What is your condition?' the King asked Hasan.

'Ill,' replied Hasan, 'but I seek to remedy that.'

'I send ships to the Islands of Wak-Wak, and sometimes they send ships to me,' said the King.

'Tomorrow one of their ships will come here,' he continued, 'and you shall embark upon it, I will have you placed on board under my protection.'

'King, may you live for ever!' said Hasan, fervently, 'I would give my life for even one glimpse of my wife!'

'Take great care, or you may be in danger beyond estimation,' warned the King. 'You are lucky that you arrived at this time; I hope that your luck will hold.'

So, next day, Hasan was sent on board one of the ships bound for the Islands of Wak-Wak, under the King's protection, and the ship set sail.

For the next ten days the ship went on, through

shark-infested seas, till its anchor was thrown out, and Hasan stepped ashore.

On the dockside there were a thousand or more beautiful divans, with cushions and fine cloths draped on them, as if a huge concourse of people were in the habit of using them to rest.

He hid behind one of the divans, and waited silently. When evening came, there arrived a great company of female soldiers, converging upon the place where the divans were arranged.

Each soldier threw herself upon one divan, and discoursed with her neighbour. They were dressed in chain-mail, with swords in their hands. Hasan saw they were all tall and most beautifully formed, notwithstanding their rough attire and warlike equipment.

They wore steel helmets, with intricate designs, and had thongs binding their legs.

Hasan waited until he saw one approach his divan, and called to her in a low voice, 'O help me, I beg you not to kill me!'

She looked at him with great blue eyes full of fire, her sword in her hand ready for action.

'Who are you?' she asked.

'My name is Hasan,' he answered. 'Take under your protection one who has lost his wife and children, and does not want to lose his life in search of them without putting up a fight!'

She was intrigued, and he heard her say, 'Hasan my son, you are fortunate you have chosen an old woman, for I fear one of my young officers would have killed you! Hide under this divan, and wait; what is to be, will be.'

Hasan concealed himself, and the time passed with stories of war and battles far too bloodthirsty for his tender heart. The female army disported themselves, and told tales and laughed loudly like the soldiers they were.

Now, the woman he had spoken to appeared in the darkness and handed him a coat of mail and chain-mail trousers just like those which the women wore, and signed to him to put them on over his own clothes. She then gave him a steel helmet and beckoned him to follow her.

He did so, and she led him to a tent which was obviously that of the commander, from the pennants fluttering outside.

He saw her, now that she was without her armour, to be old and hideous, pockmarked with smallpox, grizzled of head and bold of face. The only thing good about her was her candid blue gaze.

Appealing to her humorous eyes, Hasan begged for sanctuary. She asked him, 'How in the world did you get here, and why and how long do you expect to live, now that you have arrived?' and she slapped her hip, laughing.

Hasan answered as best he could; and she was so impressed by his replies that she promised him her protection as commander of the army. Hasan thanked his lucky stars that he had chosen her.

The commander then sent instructions to her officers to take the army out in battle order, and to rehearse for their next foray. None was to remain in the camp, under pain of death.

As soon as they had all marched away, the old woman told Hasan that she was called Shawahee, and that she was in possession of news for him.

'Your wife, of whom I have heard, is on the seventh island of the Islands of the Wak-Wak. The distance from here is very far, and fraught with danger,' she said.

'I must go, whatever the perils,' said Hasan. She nodded approvingly. 'You must go past the Island of the Hyenas, the place where the lions roar; the Island of Birds, where terrible birds of prey utter horrible cries continually; then you must pass over the Land of the Jinn, where the flames rise from the ground, and no man can live in peace. But I will take you, and we shall pass all these places, and more, till we come to a great river, and this river extends to the Islands of Wak-Wak. Do you understand the dangers?'

'I do, but I would go to the ends of the world,' said Hasan fervently, 'for I love my wife, and I believe she loves me.'

'Do you realise that you may lose your life?' asked

the female commander.

'Yes,' said Hasan stoutly, 'and if you will help me, I am ready to go now.'

'Those islands get their name from the trees which have heads fixed upon their branches, which continually raise their eyes to Heaven and cry "Wak-Wak!"' she told him. 'I will make all arrangements, and we shall go when my soldiers return.'

'So be it,' said Hasan, and prayed to Allah that he might be successful.

By dawn, the entire army returned, and Hasan heard the commander address them, and tell them that she was leading them on an expedition to the dreaded Islands of Wak-Wak. Each woman raised her spear in the air and cheered. The Commander was a popular one with the troops. Dressed in mail, Hasan left at the side of the female chief, full of courage and strength of purpose. The jingling of the harness, neighing of horses, the rattle of swords in their scabbards were music to his ears.

Sometimes they travelled by road, sometimes by sea, suffice it to tell that at long last Hasan looked upon the green Islands of Wak-Wak, where the heads, impaled upon the branches of trees, continually cried out 'Wak-Wak!' and those pitiful cries pierced the hearts of whoever heard them.

'Now, Hasan,' said the commander, pointing to a wondrous palace, 'there lies the place where your wife lives. Wear this cap of invisibility. It will take you safely into the very midst of her father's guards.

'Go, and blessings upon you.' Then she turned her troops about and departed.

Lean as a greyhound, sunburned as dark as a Moor, still as strong as when he began his search, Hasan went to the palace. It was guarded by heavily armed men, soldiers of the King of the Jaan.

But, with the magic cap, he was able to enter the gate, and penetrate to the room where, on a bed covered with a cover of gold brocade, his wife lay asleep.

After the long campaign, his gruelling marches and long rides on horseback, voyages by sea and land, Hasan felt he could have shouted aloud at seeing at long last that beautiful face.

But, having a care for his safety, he bent over the bed, and whispered in her ear, 'I am here, my Beauty of Beauties, here is Hasan, come to take you away!'

When she woke, and looked around, he took off the cap of invisibility, and she saw him.

The Bird-Maiden cried out, 'Hasan! It is not safe for you to be here! You will be killed if you are seen!'

'I have got so far without being killed, my love, and I shall get you away safely, too,' he said. He quickly told her the story of the last few months' journey.

'I never thought to see you again,' she murmured, 'it has been so long since I returned here.'

'Is it not enough that I have come?' he answered.

'I shall take you and the children away with me.'

'You cannot! It is impossible,' she said. 'You do not know how well-guarded we are. My father would never let me escape. Go now, and save yourself, forget about me.'

'You cannot take from me the spoils of my victory!' answered Hasan, boldly. 'I have won my way to you, and as you are my wife, I shall take you!'

'You must know what we would have to face, on the way back, and it may be death for you any moment now!' cried the Bird-Maiden.

Then his two sons came into the room, and knew their father, and he played with them a while.

The Queen, the Bird-Maiden's mother, then knocked on her daughter's door saying, 'What is this I hear, a man's voice? Open to me that I may punish you, for no one of the human sort may be allowed in this holiest island of all our Islands!'

So Hasan straightaway put on his cap of invisibility, and hid from the Queen's sight, and she went away satisfied that there was no one there.

That evening, as dusk came, Hasan came out of the closet of his wife's room, and said to her:

'Come, my love, you take one child and I will take the other, and we will go from here, for I am strong, and you must go with me.'

So, they each took a child in their arms, and Hasan with his cap of invisibility led her through the guards, who lay on the palace floors, in twos and threes, like sleeping dogs.

Just as they got to the palace grounds, they met an old woman.

'Let me help you,' she said. 'O daughter of the Jaan, I see your husband, who is human, though he has a cap of invisibility on his head. Take this reed, and strike it three times upon the ground, and efrits will come to bear you away.'

The Bird-Maiden thanked her, and gave her a jewel from her finger. The Bird-Maiden struck the reed three times upon the ground, and two gigantic efrits came, bowing low in homage.

'We obey the owner of the Magic Reed,' they said. 'Give us your orders and we shall perform our duty.'

'What distance is there between here and Baghdad?' asked Hasan.

'Not far, if we take you upon our shoulders,' said the efrits, and Hasan said:

'Then let us go to Baghdad, now!'

One efrit took the Bird-Maiden and one child, and Hasan was lifted upon the shoulder of the second, his younger son in his arms.

The air was filled with a strange rushing sound, the night became black, without a star in the sky, and Hasan felt himself being carried at great speed through the air.

In less time than it takes to tell, the two efrits

landed safely in Hasan's garden in Baghdad, and placed Hasan, his wife and the children safely on the ground.

Dismissing the efrits, Hasan loudly knocked on his own door, calling his mother with joyful anticipation. His wife, standing beside him, looked at him with her eyes shining with love.

In a few moments he heard the bolts being drawn, and his mother opened the door.

The moment she saw them, the old woman shrieked with happiness. Then she clasped them in her arms, one by one. Hasan vowed to himself that never again would he ever leave his home, or his family. His wife went to her own apartments, and dressed herself and the children in their finest clothes.

'Husband,' said she, when Hasan went in to her, 'I swear I have learned by being parted from you that I love you with all my heart, and will never leave you again. Light the fire,' she continued and when he did so, she dropped the feather robe into the flames. Then she returned shyly to Hasan's arms.

Within a few weeks, Hasan once more became the Goldsmith of Basra, and they lived happily the rest of their lives.

The Slowest May Win the Race

The hare and the tortoise, according to Aesop, ran a race because the hare boasted about his speed, but the tortoise won because of his steady plodding. But the theme of the animal race in which the slower wins has been presented among all manner of people to illustrate a variety of supposed truths. In a Sinhalese tale it is a lion and a tortoise, and the latter arranges with his brother to appear at the opposite side of a river bearing a flower in token of identity. Far from there being a virtue in plodding, the slower creature here uses only his wits. In Madagascar, a chameleon actually makes a wild hog carry him in its mane. Every time the unwitting hog stopped, the chameleon leapt upon the grass a little way ahead and seemed to be in front.

The story has even travelled as far as Fiji, where a crane and a crab are in competition. This time the crane stops every now and then at a crab-hole and hears the buzzing which he takes for that of his challenger. The message is that anything may be accomplished by trusting to the co-operation of relatives.

Here is the Siamese presentation, collected in Thailand by Adolf Bastian.

THE GARUDA – MAGICAL bird of Vishnu – was hungry as, one day, he flew over a lake and saw a tortoise in it. The tortoise diverted his interest by suggesting that, before being eaten up, they should run a race to see who was the faster.

The magnificent bird agreed, and rose high into the air, ready to fly. While he was doing that, the tortoise collected all his friends and relatives – all the living tortoises – and placed them in rows of 100, of 1,000, of 10,000, of 100,000, of a million and of ten million, so that they covered every inch of the ground.

When he was ready, the tortoise called out:

'I am ready to start. Your Highness may go through the air, while I shall move by water, and we shall see who is the winner. The wager is that if I lose, you will be able to eat me up.'

Now the Garuda flew with all his might, and then stopped and called to the tortoise. And, whichever direction he flew, a tortoise always answered him, from somewhere ahead. He even flew as far as the great mountain, the Himaphan. At last he had to tell the tortoise that he had been outraced, and he returned, baffled, to his home, the *rathal* tree, to rest.

The Three Imposters

One hundred years before the European invention of printing, Prince Manuel, nephew of the Spanish King Alfonso the Wise, wrote The Fifty Pleasant Stories, *one of the real gems of early Spanish literature. He died in 1347, and the book was not printed until over two hundred years afterwards, when it appeared in Seville. It lay forgotten until the Madrid edition of 1642, and these two impressions are today among the rarest books in the world. After nearly another two centuries it came out in Stuttgart (1839) and then in Paris the following year. This story, 'A King and Three Imposters', is said by Prince Manuel to come from a Moorish source. It is, of course, undoubtedly the basis of Hans Christian Andersen's 'The Emperor's New Clothes'.*

THREE IMPOSTERS CAME to a king and told him that they were weavers, and could produce a cloth of such a strange kind that a legitimate son of his father could see it, but nobody else could, even if they were believed to be legitimate.

Now the King was much pleased at this, thinking that by this means he would be able to distinguish those who were the sons of their supposed fathers from those who were not. So he ordered a palace to be set aside for the making of this cloth. The three men, to convince him that they were genuine and sincere, agreed to be shut up in this building until the cloth had been made; and this satisfied the King.

The weavers were given a large quantity of gold, silver and silk and many other things to work with. They set up their looms in the palace and pretended that they were working all day at the cloth.

After some days, one of the men went to the King and told him that the cloth had been started, and he told him all kinds of things about it, and asked him to visit them, but asked that he should come alone.

The King was very pleased, but thought that he would get another opinion of the magical fabric first, so he sent the Lord Chamberlain to have a look. The Lord Chamberlain duly went and could see nothing, but he dared not admit that the wonderful cloth was invisible to him, so he returned to the King and said that he had really seen it.

The King then sent someone else, and received the same report. Now the King decided to see for himself.

When he entered the Palace, the King found the men there, and they described the cloth in detail, including its design. They all agreed on these details, and even the origin and method of making of the cloth. The King could not see anything at all, for there was no cloth there. But he began to feel very uneasy, fearing that he might not be the true son of the King who was supposed to be his father. 'If *I* cannot see it,' he thought, 'I might have to lose my kingdom, which depends upon inheritance.' So he started to praise the cloth, and repeated the details which the imposters had outlined.

When he returned to his own palace, the King continued to speak of the cloth as if it were real, though at the same time he inwardly suspected that something was wrong.

After a few days, the monarch asked his Wakil, the officer of justice, to go and see the cloth. Exactly the same thing happened to the Wakil. He went into the palace of the weavers, who described the pattern, though he could see nothing of any cloth of any kind. Naturally the unhappy Wakil immediately imagined that he could not be the true son of his father, and that that must be the cause of the material remaining invisible to him. Fearing that the discovery of this fact about him would mean the loss of his important position, the Wakil set about praising the non-existent cloth in even more extravagant terms than the King and the Lord Chamberlain.

He went back to the King, and told him that he had, indeed, viewed the cloth, and that it was the most extraordinary tissue in the world. The King was deeply distressed: there could now, he thought, be no doubt that he himself was not the offspring of his father. But he hastened to agree with the rapturous descriptions of the wondrous fabric brought him by the law officer. And he did not forget to add unstinted praise for the inspired workmen who were weaving it.

The King continued to send people to see the cloth, and they, not unnaturally, all came back to him with the same impressions as everyone else.

This tale continued in just the same way until the King was told that the cloth was finished. He ordered that a great feast be prepared, where everyone should be dressed in clothes made from the miraculous material. The weavers thereupon presented themselves, with 'some of the cloth' rolled in fine linen, and asked his Majesty how much would be required; and the King told them the quantity and what kind of clothes were to be made.

The feast day arrived, and the clothes were reported to be complete. The weavers came to the King with the magic robe which he himself was to wear. The King, of course, did not dare to say that he could not see it, or even feel it.

Now the imposters pretended to dress the King in his new clothes; and he mounted his horse and rode into the city. Luckily it was summer time! People who saw the King pass were very surprised at what they beheld. But word had got around that only the illegitimate were unable to see the cloth, so people kept their distress and amazement to themselves.

All of them did, in fact, except a black man who was among those lining the streets. He immediately approached the King and said:

'Sire, it is of no interest to me whose son I am. So I can tell you that in fact you are riding about without any clothes on!'

At first the King struck the black a blow, saying that he must be illegitimate and that was why the cloth was invisible to him. But other people, once the spell of silence and fear had been broken, saw that it was true, and said the same. Even the King and his court now realized that they had been tricked.

The false weavers, of course, when they were sought, were found to have fled with the things which the King had given them 'to make the cloth from'.

Occasion

It is often claimed that folktales represent survivals of ancient religious beliefs. This story either gives the lie to that suggestion – since it has no identifiable Christian message – or else it supports it if it represents some other, more ancient belief-system. How the individual can prevail over and dominate a spiritual power, upon which he is shown in the tale itself to depend for the benefits of the Hereafter, is justified, can perhaps only be explained by the wish-fulfilment factor.

This account, although not the only example of its kind, is taken from Sicilian folklore.

THERE WAS ONCE an orphan, named 'Occasion', who was taken in, from pity, by a certain couple. When he was grown up, the foster-parents said:

'Well, Occasion, is it not time that you supported yourself, as you are now a man?'

Occasion set off on his travels, and journeyed until he became completely exhausted and ragged. He arrived at an inn, where he asked to become a servant, in exchange for nothing more than a piece of bread for wages.

The innkeeper and his wife, Rosella, took him in, and he worked so well that they adopted him. When they died he inherited the inn.

When Occasion took over the establishment he announced: 'Whoever should come to Occasion's Inn can have food for nothing.'

Jesus and St Thomas heard about this, and the latter said that he did not believe it, and would only credit it if he touched it with his hands. They went and ate and drank and were well entertained by Occasion.

Before leaving, St Thomas asked whether Occasion would like a favour from the Master. Occasion said that he could not get any figs from his tree, as boys climbed up it and stole them. 'I would like this favour,' he asked, 'that whenever anyone climbs this tree, he just stays there until I allow him down.'

The request was granted. Occasion found that all

the boys who climbed the tree were stuck fast, and he punished them when they tried to steal his fruit, and they stole no more.

Occasion's money was coming to an end as time passed. So he called a carpenter and had him make a bottle from the wood of the fig-tree. The power of this bottle was that whoever was shut in it could not get out.

Then Death came to Occasion, for he was now very old.

Occasion said:

'I am ready to go, but do me a favour. There is a fly in this wine bottle. Get it out for me before I drink, and then I will come with you.'

Death went into the bottle, and Occasion put it in his wallet, saying, 'Stay a while with me.'

Now, since Death was imprisoned, nobody died; there were old men with long white beards everywhere.

The disciples came to hear of this and went to the Master again and again. Eventually he visited Occasion and complained.

Occasion said:

'If you give me a place in paradise, I will let Death out.'

The Lord thought: 'If I do not agree, he will give us no peace.' So he granted the request.

So people were allowed to die, and Occasion had

some years of his own life left.

This is why there is a saying: 'There is no death without Occasion.'

FINIS